Francis Frith's
SOUTH DEVON LIVING MEMORIES

PHOTOGRAPHIC MEMORIES

Francis Frith's
SOUTH DEVON
LIVING MEMORIES

◆

Dennis Needham

FRITH
BOOK CO

First published in the United Kingdom in 2000 by
Frith Book Company Ltd

Hardback Edition 2000
ISBN 1-85937-168-x

Paperback Edition 2002
ISBN 1-85937-609-6

British Library Cataloguing in Publication Data

Francis Frith's South Devon Living Memories
Dennis Needham

Frith Book Company Ltd
Frith's Barn, Teffont,
Salisbury, Wiltshire SP3 5QP
Tel: +44 (0) 1722 716 376
Email: info@francisfrith.co.uk
www.francisfrith.co.uk

Printed and bound in Great Britain

Contents

Francis Frith: Victorian Pioneer   7

Frith's Archive - A Unique Legacy   10

South Devon Living Memories
An Introduction   12

The Eastern Side   16

The Northern Areas   38

Dartmoor and its Environs   51

The Torbay Area   65

The West of the County   87

Index   115

Free Mounted Print Voucher   *119*

FRANCIS FRITH: *Victorian Pioneer*

FRANCIS FRITH, Victorian founder of the world-famous photographic archive, was a complex and fascinating man. A devout Quaker and a highly successful Victorian businessman, he was both philosophic by nature and pioneering in outlook.

By 1855 Francis Frith had already established a wholesale grocery business in Liverpool, and sold it for the astonishing sum of £200,000, which is the equivalent today of over £15,000,000. Now a multi-millionaire, he was able to indulge his passion for travel. As a child he had pored over travel books written by early explorers, and his fancy and imagination had been stirred by family holidays to the sublime mountain regions of Wales and Scotland. 'What a land of spirit-stirring and enriching scenes and places!' he had written. He was to return to these scenes of grandeur in later years to 'recapture the thousands of vivid and tender memories', but with a different purpose. Now in his thirties, and captivated by the new science of photography, Frith set out on a series of pioneering journeys to the Nile regions that occupied him from 1856 until 1860.

INTRIGUE AND ADVENTURE

He took with him on his travels a specially-designed wicker carriage that acted as both dark-room and sleeping chamber. These far-flung journeys were packed with intrigue and adventure. In his life story, written when he was sixty-three, Frith tells of being held captive by bandits, and of fighting 'an awful midnight battle to the very point of surrender with a deadly pack of hungry, wild dogs'. Sporting flowing Arab costume, Frith arrived at Akaba by camel seventy years before Lawrence, where he encountered 'desert princes and rival sheikhs, blazing with jewel-hilted swords'.

During these extraordinary adventures he was assiduously exploring the desert regions bordering the Nile and patiently recording the antiquities and peoples with his camera. He was the first photographer to venture beyond the sixth cataract. Africa was still the mysterious 'Dark Continent', and Stanley and Livingstone's historic meeting was a decade into the future. The conditions for picture taking confound belief. He laboured for hours in his wicker dark-room in the sweltering heat of the desert, while the volatile chemicals fizzed dangerously in their trays. Often he was forced to work in remote tombs and caves where conditions

were cooler. Back in London he exhibited his photographs and was 'rapturously cheered' by members of the Royal Society. His reputation as a photographer was made overnight. An eminent modern historian has likened their impact on the population of the time to that on our own generation of the first photographs taken on the surface of the moon.

VENTURE OF A LIFE-TIME

Characteristically, Frith quickly spotted the opportunity to create a new business as a specialist publisher of photographs. He lived in an era of immense and sometimes violent change. For the poor in the early part of Victoria's reign work was a drudge and the hours long, and people had precious little free time to enjoy themselves.

Most had no transport other than a cart or gig at their disposal, and had not travelled far beyond the boundaries of their own town or village. However, by the 1870s, the railways had threaded their way across the country, and Bank Holidays and half-day Saturdays had been made obligatory by Act of Parliament. All of a sudden the ordinary working man and his family were able to enjoy days out and see a little more of the world.

With characteristic business acumen, Francis Frith foresaw that these new tourists would enjoy having souvenirs to commemorate their days out. In 1860 he married Mary Ann Rosling and set out with the intention of photographing every city, town and village in Britain. For the next thirty years he travelled the country by train and by pony and trap, producing fine photographs of seaside resorts and beauty spots that were keenly bought by millions of Victorians. These prints were painstakingly pasted into family albums and pored over during the dark nights of winter, rekindling precious memories of summer excursions.

THE RISE OF FRITH & CO

Frith's studio was soon supplying retail shops all over the country. To meet the demand he gathered about him a small team of photographers, and published the work of independent artist-photographers of the calibre of Roger Fenton and Francis Bedford. In order to gain some understanding of the scale of Frith's business one only has to look at the catalogue issued by Frith & Co in 1886: it

runs to some 670 pages, listing not only many thousands of views of the British Isles but also many photographs of most European countries, and China, Japan, the USA and Canada – note the sample page shown above from the hand-written *Frith & Co* ledgers detailing pictures taken. By 1890 Frith had created the greatest specialist photographic publishing company in the world, with over 2,000 outlets – more than the combined number that Boots and WH Smith have today! The picture on the right shows the *Frith & Co* display board at Ingleton in the Yorkshire Dales. Beautifully constructed with mahogany frame and gilt inserts, it could display up to a dozen local scenes.

POSTCARD BONANZA

The ever-popular holiday postcard we know today took many years to develop. In 1870 the Post Office issued the first plain cards, with a pre-printed stamp on one face. In 1894 they allowed other publishers' cards to be sent through the mail with an attached adhesive halfpenny stamp. Demand grew rapidly, and in 1895 a new size of postcard

was permitted called the court card, but there was little room for illustration. In 1899, a year after Frith's death, a new card measuring 5.5 x 3.5 inches became the standard format, but it was not until 1902 that the divided back came into being, with address and message on one face and a full-size illustration on the other. *Frith & Co* were in the vanguard of postcard development, and Frith's sons Eustace and Cyril continued their father's monumental task, expanding the number of views offered to the public and recording more and more places in Britain, as the coasts and countryside were opened up to mass travel.

Francis Frith died in 1898 at his villa in Cannes, his great project still growing. The archive he created continued in business for another seventy years. By 1970 it contained over a third of a million pictures of 7,000 cities, towns and villages. The massive photographic record Frith has left to us stands as a living monument to a special and very remarkable man.

Frith's Archive: *A Unique Legacy*

FRANCIS FRITH'S legacy to us today is of immense significance and value, for the magnificent archive of evocative photographs he created provides a unique record of change in 7,000 cities, towns and villages throughout Britain over a century and more. Frith and his fellow studio photographers revisited locations many times down the years to update their views, compiling for us an enthralling and colourful pageant of British life and character.

We tend to think of Frith's sepia views of Britain as nostalgic, for most of us use them to conjure up memories of places in our own lives with which we have family associations. It often makes us forget that to Francis Frith they were records of daily life as it was actually being lived in the cities, towns and villages of his day. The Victorian age was one of great and often bewildering change for ordinary people, and though the pictures evoke an impression of slower times, life was as busy and hectic as it is today.

We are fortunate that Frith was a photographer of the people, dedicated to recording the minutiae of everyday life. For it is this sheer wealth of visual data, the painstaking chronicle of changes in dress, transport, street layouts, buildings, housing, engineering and landscape that captivates us so much today. His remarkable images offer us a powerful link with the past and with the lives of our ancestors.

TODAY'S TECHNOLOGY

Computers have now made it possible for Frith's many thousands of images to be accessed almost instantly. In the Frith archive today, each photograph is carefully 'digitised' then stored on a CD Rom. Frith archivists can locate a single photograph amongst thousands within seconds. Views can be catalogued and sorted under a variety of categories of place and content to the immediate benefit of researchers. Inexpensive reference prints can be created for them at the touch of a mouse button, and a wide range of books and other printed materials assembled and published for a wider, more general readership - in the next twelve months over a hundred Frith local history titles will be published! The day-to-

THE FRANCIS FRITH COLLECTION
Photographic publishers since 1860

HOME | PHOTO SEARCH | BOOKS | PORTFOLIO | GALLERY   MY CART
Products | History | Other Collections | Contact us | Help?

your town, your village

365,000 photographs of 7,000 towns and villages, taken between 1860 & 1970.

The Frith Archive
The Frith Archive is the remarkable legacy of its energetic and visionary founder. Today, the Frith archive is the only nationally important archive of its kind still in private ownership.

The Collection is world-renowned for the extraordinary quality of its images.

The Gallery
This month The Frith Gallery features images from "Frith's Egypt".

News...
Image update complete.
An additional 5,000 images have been added and the quality of all images has now been improved.

Sample chapters available.
The first selection of sample chapters from the Frith Book Co.'s extensive range is now available. All are offered in Pdf format for easy downloading and viewing.

explore FRITH
Search thousands of photographs from one of the worlds' great archives.

Town search

County search
Select a county

the FRITHgallery

See Frith at www.francisfrith.co.uk

day workings of the archive are very different from how they were in Francis Frith's time: imagine the herculean task of sorting through eleven tons of glass negatives as Frith had to do to locate a particular sequence of pictures! Yet the archive still prides itself on maintaining the same high standards of excellence laid down by Francis Frith, including the painstaking cataloguing and indexing of every view.

It is curious to reflect on how the internet now allows researchers in America and elsewhere greater instant access to the archive than Frith himself ever enjoyed. Many thousands of individual views can be called up on screen within seconds on one of the Frith internet sites, enabling people living continents away to revisit the streets of their ancestral home town, or view places in Britain where they have enjoyed holidays. Many overseas researchers welcome the chance to view special theme selections, such as transport, sports, costume and ancient monuments.

We are certain that Francis Frith would have heartily approved of these modern developments, for he himself was always working at the very limits of Victorian photographic technology.

THE VALUE OF THE ARCHIVE TODAY

Because of the benefits brought by the computer, Frith's images are increasingly studied by social historians, by researchers into genealogy and ancestory, by architects, town planners, and by teachers and schoolchildren involved in local history projects. In addition, the archive offers every one of us a unique opportunity to examine the places where we and our families have lived and worked down the years. Immensely successful in Frith's own era, the archive is now, a century and more on, entering a new phase of popularity.

THE PAST IN TUNE WITH THE FUTURE

Historians consider the Francis Frith Collection to be of prime national importance. It is the only archive of its kind remaining in private ownership and has been valued at a million pounds. However, this figure is now rapidly increasing as digital technology enables more and more people around the world to enjoy its benefits.

Francis Frith's archive is now housed in an historic timber barn in the beautiful village of Teffont in Wiltshire. Its founder would not recognize the archive office as it is today. In place of the many thousands of dusty boxes containing glass plate negatives and an all-pervading odour of photographic chemicals, there are now ranks of computer screens. He would be amazed to watch his images travelling round the world at unimaginable speeds through network and internet lines.

The archive's future is both bright and exciting. Francis Frith, with his unshakeable belief in making photographs available to the greatest number of people, would undoubtedly approve of what is being done today with his lifetime's work. His photographs, depicting our shared past, are now bringing pleasure and enlightenment to millions around the world a century and more after his death.

SOUTH DEVON LIVING MEMORIES
an introduction

AS ONE OF the most popular holiday destinations in England, south Devon can labour under a huge burden of visitors for much of the summer. Apart from a temperate climate, one of the main attractions is the sheer quality of its countryside. Whilst many will seek out the beaches and gently soak up the sun all day long, the more enterprising will be looking out for treasures only lightly hidden. For south Devon is nothing without its narrow lanes leading to its pretty villages; they are still relatively isolated even today. They were much more so after the last war, before the car really established itself as omnipotent.

And yet, there is the paradox. Most of Devon's roads were built to suit the horse and cart. Over the years, they have not changed much either. The percentage of dual carriageway in this area is an infinitesimal part of the total road miles; so if you want to explore where our photographer visited, be prepared to take your time. But surely, time is what you have. Although most of the views contained within these covers were taken

within living memory, that era was so different. The hustle and bustle of life today, the frenetic pace at which we live would, in those days, be part of some Orwellian nightmare. Who would have conceived - who would have believed - the way life has become so complicated? Yet this is Devon. Locals will tell you that living in this area is one coat warmer and one gear lower than life up-country. That definition, incidentally, seems to apply to anyone who lives beyond the county line.

This volume is divided into five chapters. Within each of these, the pictures are arranged so that, using a car to visit the locations, they will follow more or less sequentially.

The east of the county is the least Devonian, possibly because it is the first area to be reached by incomers. But, as you will discover within the chapter, the area was beautiful half a century ago - and still is today. With the exception of Exmouth, the holiday towns have lost their rail connections and the road traffic has grown to replace it. But the disappearance of the railway has not been matched by an improvement in roads.

As you journey around the area, history as well as beauty will leap out at you. Apart from the timeless views as confirmed by these pages, you will discover a world that manages to keep itself well hidden. Budleigh Salterton is a good example. It was on the sea wall here that Sir John Millais painted his famous picture 'The Boyhood of Raleigh'. It was in this very area that Sir Walter grew up. P G Wodehouse and Noel Coward were to be seen regularly in the town at the time our photographers were active. Or take Honiton - a charming town, as our views will attest. But how many people associate that delicate delight known as Honiton lace with the town? Yes, this is where it used to be made. Axminster looked quite stunning according to the views we reproduce here - and Axminster carpets are made here to this day. Exeter was a Roman fort once upon a time, and has since grown to be a splendidly mature city full of ancient buildings and fascinating streets. A small flavour of this most agreeable place will be gleaned from the illustration reproduced here.

It is not exactly an oxymoron to talk about the north of south Devon. Some of the most lush and fertile parts of the county can be found within this area. A bright red soil marks the fields here, and the cattle that graze the fields produce milk from which the glorious Devonshire cream is made. There are attractive towns such as Tiverton and Okehampton; the latter, nestling at the foot of Dartmoor, is the main centre for exploration of the Moor. But above all it is the unspoilt countryside around this region that really marks it out as special. As you drive around, looking at the pictures in this chapter, you will come to appreciate just how little things have changed around here.

We then move to Dartmoor, that most forbidding of areas: dark, treacherous bogs seize the unwary, and mists and fog descend so quickly, often from a clear blue sky, that many a hiker has been lost for hours - days even - before stumbling into some welcome area of civilisation. At Princetown is the prison that used to strike terror into the heart of many an old lag. Dartmoor was the place

EXMOUTH, PROMENADE GARDENS c1950

they all hoped to avoid. If you ever got over the walls, the Moor was a dangerous enemy that had to be conquered before real freedom was reached.

Yet, treated with only a modicum of respect, Dartmoor is a simply wonderful place. Here, you can walk for hours without seeing another human being. The only company you are likely to have are a few north of the moor around Okehampton. As you will see from the chapter on this wilderness, the views and locations are stunningly beautiful. People who choose to live high on the Moor have to be of a particular kind. Patience and fortitude are two of the qualities most needed. Be sure that at some stage in the winter months, you will be cut off from the world. Perhaps the snow

DARTMEET c1960 D5007

Dartmoor sheep, a hardy breed especially adapted to life in the Moor. The views are out of this world, and one of England's last great wildernesses can be enjoyed to the limit. But there is one blight on the Moor. The army, as is their wont, have colonised a substantial corner of it on which to practice their manoeuvres. There is some perverse law of nature which demands that these people select the most beautiful corners of our green and pleasant land for their games. The areas they use are out of bounds. They fire live ammunition too, so watch for the red flags flying around the area they use: mainly to the or ice will bring down power and telephone cables and you will be completely isolated.

South of the Moor is Torbay, the premier holiday area. It teems with visitors for much of the year as hoteliers push hard to fill their vast spaces out of season. The rail network still reaches here and holidaymakers still arrive by train, albeit not in the quantities of days gone by. The bottleneck that was the Newton Abbot to Kingswear line after the war used to see trains backed up well beyond Exeter, sometimes reaching the Somerset border. Delays were measured in hours then, not the minutes of today.

The west of south Devon is dominated by the city of Plymouth, and the surrounding towns and villages have grown to accommodate a population that increasingly likes to live somewhere special and commute. The lack of good roads and an almost non-existent rail service means that people generally stick to somewhere within easy access of the (few) main roads. This has left most of the villages we visit in this chapter completely recognisable today. Changes generally have been of a cosmetic nature, and the closure of both village shops and pubs indicate that the incidence of incomers is spasmodic to say the least.

The small towns - Tavistock and Ivybridge - and the dozens of pretty little villages - Milton Combe is one of the best - offer delight and fascination in equal measure. Vast road developments and the building of retail parks has left south Devon relatively unaffected. Thus, where the old has been swept away up-country in a frenzy of re-development, this has not happened in south Devon. Therefore, you can visit Plymouth and find so much of the old still there to delight. The Luftwaffe were efficient demolition contractors during the war, but they missed much of the real historic heart of the city. You can walk the same streets as those walked by Drake, Raleigh and Frobisher, and see the same views they saw. Stand where the Pilgrim Fathers stood for the last time on English soil and see where they slept for their final night here. Pages from the history books leap vividly to life.

One of the great pleasures of jaunts such as this is to carry this volume along with you. Enjoy the experience of working out just where our photographer set up his equipment half a century ago. As you photograph the same view with your automatic camera, picture the somewhat primitive equipment those earlier photographers carried. Marvel at how little our green and pleasant land has changed during the intervening years. Or perhaps frown at the wanton destruction of the eye-pleasing views seen in this book, and try to decide how such architectural nightmares that sometimes stand in their place ever came to be built. Wonder at the acres of green fields that have disappeared under a welter of bricks and concrete.

KINGSWEAR, GENERAL VIEW c1960 K34001

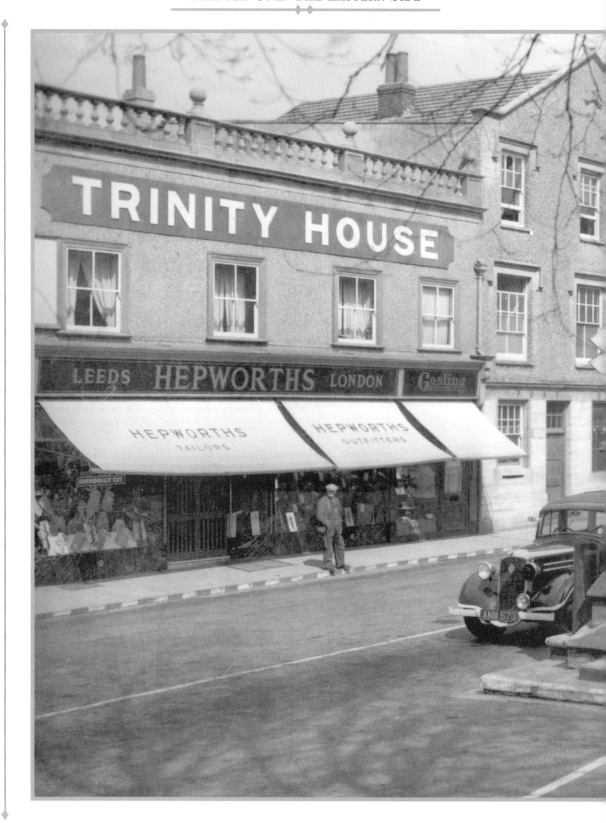

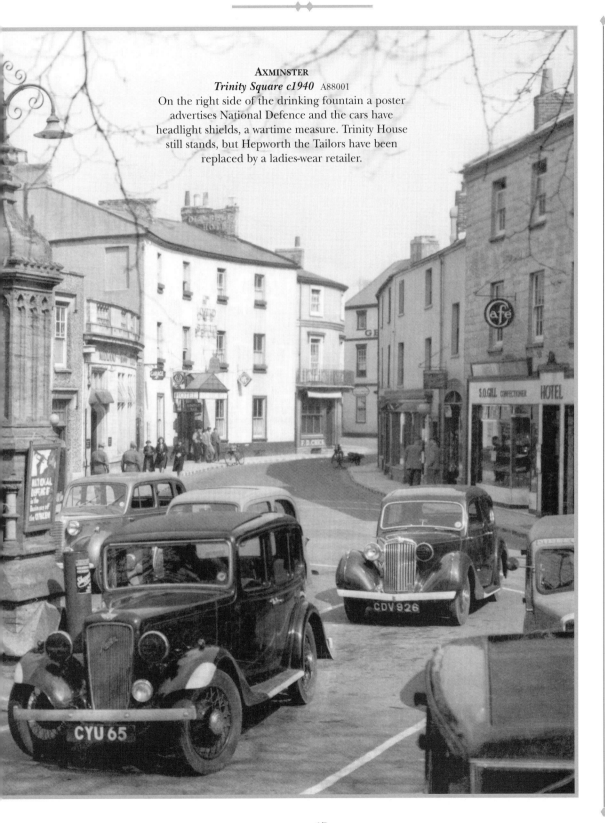

AXMINSTER
Trinity Square c1940 A88001
On the right side of the drinking fountain a poster advertises National Defence and the cars have headlight shields, a wartime measure. Trinity House still stands, but Hepworth the Tailors have been replaced by a ladies-wear retailer.

AXMINSTER, THE SQUARE c1940 A88012
Here we see the town's grocers as they were before supermarkets rampaged through into our consciousness. The bicycle outside would be used by the errand boy to deliver customers' orders.

MEMBURY, THE VILLAGE c1955 M61503
The Red Lion pub has gone the way of many a village tavern: converted to a home. It is still known as Red Lion House and, intriguingly, the post and framework holding the sign are still there. The Bedford van has been consigned to the scrap heap, but the church of St John the Baptist still thrives.

YARCOMBE, THE CHURCH AND THE YARCOMBE INN c1960 Y19059
Yarcombe was once a sleepy hamlet, but when the main A30 was cut in the early 19th century, heavy traffic arrived. On this sharp bend, looking towards Chard, stands The Yarcombe Inn. This place has slaked the thirst and provided shelter for many a traveller over the years. At one time it would have been the Church House. The church is dedicated to St John the Baptist and is mainly of the 15th century.

OFFWELL, THE VILLAGE c1960 O60007
The substantial building to the right is a Church of England Voluntary Controlled Primary School, and the column on the corner marks the presence of the Copleston family here, even before Norman times. The trees to the left have been felled, giving a view of St Mary's church.

HONITON, HIGH STREET c1955 H111039

Once on the main London to Exeter road, this wide straight street has Roman origins. Little has changed (apart from the makes of the cars,) although the individual businesses are not the same. On the left, the first building is the attractive Manor House. On the right, note the petrol hoses fixed to cranes on the building walls. The National Benzole fuel logo is also fixed above them.

HONITON, HIGH STREET c1955 H111024

This view looks towards Exeter. The Globe Inn still stands, but is converted to non-licensed use. The thatched building a little further along is the Pig and Barrow pub.

GITTISHAM, THE STREAM C1965 G136003
Dozens of thatched cottages make up this gorgeous village. The posts to the left have been replaced by a stone wall. This is a flood prevention measure: several houses just beyond the bridge used to move their furniture upstairs regularly in times of heavy rain, preparing for the inevitable. Crabbs Cottage to the right is in a much better state of repair today.

OTTERY ST MARY, BROAD STREET C1955 O28027
The essential structure of this corner has changed little in half a century. On the post to the left, a sign points to 'Public Lavatories', a word that has gone almost completely out of use today. The road sign above was provided by the AA, who, together with the RAC, erected most of our road signs for many years.

OTTERY ST MARY
The Weir Pool c1960 O28034
Whilst the camera does not lie, it certainly misleads. All around this seemingly idyllic location are factories and businesses. The scene is still charming though, and is unchanged today, save for the fact that the health and safety police have insisted that railings be fixed all around.

ROCKBEARE, THE POST OFFICE c1960 R257008

Rockbeare has suffered - since this picture was taken - by becoming a dormitory village for Exeter: a desirable place to live. Consequently, much of what was is now surrounded by 'little boxes' loved by only those who own them. Scenes like this are now literally a thing of the past.

WOODBURY, THE VILLAGE c1955 W129009

At the top end of the village, half a century on, the pleasant thatched building has gone, replaced by a modern house set back from the road. Next door are the Church Rooms. The shop (left) is no more, but the village pump is still in place.

WOODBURY, THE CHURCH c1965 W129022
St Swithin's was built in 1409 and dominates this village. Note the mini. Its suffix letter is 'D', making it first registered in Devon (TT registration mark) in 1966.

WOODBURY, THE VILLAGE c1955 W129020
The carriageway surface has been improved and white lines added. Again, the exact date of this view must be open to question, as the car in view is a Mini: they were not introduced until August 1959.

EXETER, THE CATHEDRAL c1955 E48011
If this looks magnificent, then looks do not deceive. The gorgeous west front of Exeter Cathedral is but a taster for what lies behind the door. The work here dates from 1329-42, although there are some Norman parts to be found. This study illustrates the essentially timeless nature of our great ecclesiastical buildings: only cars and fashions change.

EXETER, THE CATHEDRAL c1955 E48028
This view can now no longer be seen. Extensive building has taken place in this area, replacing the buildings flattened in the war. An 'O' model Bedford tipper truck is in the foreground. These lorries were the workhorses of the immediate post-war period. Here, they would have been employed removing demolition rubbish to the tip and returning with whatever building materials were available at the time.

EXETER, THE GUILDHALL c1955 E48006

TOPSHAM, DUTCH HOUSES, THE STRAND c1965 T59007

EXETER
The Guildhall c1955

After the cathedral, this is probably the best (and oldest) building in town. It is of the 13th century, rebuilt a hundred years later. The portico overhanging High Street was added during the reign of Queen Elizabeth I. The Turks Head Hotel next door is also ancient. The decorated iron standards that once carried both tram wires and street lighting have been replaced, but the clock above the jeweller's H Samuel hangs there to this day.

◆

TOPSHAM
Dutch Houses, The Strand c1965

Views like this are still available in Topsham, where 20th-century building has been minimal. There is a strong Dutch influence in much of the housing, especially here on the Strand. Dutch trading ships brought in bricks as ballast, and these were used by the local merchants with Dutch architecture in mind.

EXMOUTH, PROMENADE GARDENS C1950 E52020

EXMOUTH
Promenade Gardens c1950
This popular resort has long attracted visitors from all over the UK. It is also a place where the city of Exeter relaxes. The cars along the front are a delightful example of motoring at the time. Wartime austerity is still plainly evident.

◆

EXMOUTH
The Harbour Entrance c1965
The swing bridge over the entrance carries Shelly Road across the water. Today, Exmouth is mainly a fishing port, but when this view was taken, the railway still penetrated to service shipping at the quay. The boat in the foreground appears to be preparing to load passengers for a trip around the bay.

EXMOUTH, THE HARBOUR ENTRANCE C1965 E52033

LITTLEHAM, SANDY BAY HOLIDAY PARK c1960 L57030

LITTLEHAM
Sandy Bay Holiday Park c1960
This park still exists, but is much more formalised. It is but a short walk to the beach at Sandy Bay, but this idyll is sometimes a less than pleasant one. Just out of camera view, the Royal Marines have a shooting range; when they are there, it sounds as though war has broken out.

◆

LITTLEHAM,
Littleham Road c1965
This view is instantly recognisable today. The main change is that the telephone box has been removed from its perilous location in the middle of the road. Shop fascias have changed as new owners take over - the one behind the phone box is a motor spares shop, and Lloyds Bank has become a post office.

LITTLEHAM, LITTLEHAM ROAD c1965 L57068

BUDLEIGH SALTERTON, SOUTHLANDS HOTEL c1960 B243043
This is a view typical of its day. Then, holidaymakers caught the train to English seaside resorts and stayed in places like this. Today, they fly to continental resorts, and gracious places such as these are replaced by self-catering apartments.

OTTERTON, THE VILLAGE c1960 O27045
Pleasant and timeless: that describes so many Devon villages. There have been cosmetic changes here, but little else. The post office has gone, and the building is now incorporated into the property next door, complete with thatch. The electricity wires have also gone. It is unusual that the village has not lost its post office: it has been re-located by the local pub, and is now known as Arkwrights Stores. At our last visit, there was no sign of Ronnie Barker in his brown overall or David Jason on his bike.

NEWTON POPPLEFORD, MAIN STREET c1965 N82069
Today, traffic roars along this street, which is the A3052 from Exeter to Sidmouth and beyond. Otherwise, the view is essentially unchanged.

NEWTON POPPLEFORD, THE VILLAGE c1965 N82075
You will be hard-pressed to locate this scene today, although much does still exist. The Turks Head inn is replaced by new houses, and the road is behind the bank to the right. Now well shielded by trees, the building to the left, Wayside, has a roof-high tree where, in this view, a small shrub to the right of the porch can be seen. The vehicle used to be standard issue to the disabled, and was a singularly unstable machine.

SIDMOUTH, CENTRAL PROMENADE c1955 S129089

Sidmouth is still popular today with discerning holidaymakers. The sea-front buildings to the right are all now listed as fine examples of Victorian and Edwardian frontages.

SIDFORD, CHURCH STREET c1955 S128021

Cattle ambling along this street now would be quickly mown down by traffic. The wall to the left belongs to St Peter's Church and is now half the height. The garage exists, but the petrol pumps have moved. Across the road, the guest house has become The Salty Monk Hotel.

BEER, SEA HILL c1965 B55060
This is another timeless view. Fishermen still put out from here trying to eke out a living from the relentless sea.

BRANSCOMBE, THE SEA SHANTY c1940 B188003

Where the beach huts stand, wartime shore defences including a block-house were built, the latter not removed until the 1980s. The Sea Shanty has been completely rebuilt, but in the style we see and using stone reclaimed from the demolition. The houses up the hill were coastguards' and customs' properties, now for holiday hire.

COLYTON, CHURCH STREET c1965 C110012

The White Hart Inn is now a private house called - with a fine sense of tradition - White Hart. The octagonal lantern atop the parish church - St Andrew's - is 15th-century.

COLYTON, THE OLD CHURCH HOUSE c1955 C110009
Colyton is only a small place, but is blessed with many ancient buildings, this being one of them. The render from the face has now gone, and the original stonework has been revealed. But next door, the building on the right has had much of its lower half covered by boarding.

SHUTE, OLD SHUTE HOUSE c1955 S358009

This delightful old place is now in the care of the National Trust. It is one of the most important surviving un-fortified manor houses from the Middle Ages. Work started in 1380, and the house was completed by the end of the 16th century. Some of it was demolished two hundred years ago, but plenty survives. There are late Gothic windows and a Tudor gatehouse to see.

KILMINGTON, THE POST OFFICE c1960 K23007

The shop to the left is now a private dwelling called Stanley House. Just out of shot to the left the post office can be found, a rural sub-post office that continues to survive even in today's harsh business climate.

KILMINGTON, THE VILLAGE c1960 K23008

A most attractive village, Kilmington retains much of its charm to this day. The pole by the telephone box has gone, and the darker shaded wall has given way to a drive. Trees shroud the housing: otherwise, the view here has altered little.

HOLCOMBE ROGUS, THE CHURCH AND THE VICARAGE c1960 H243038

An attractive village surrounded by hills and only a mile or so from the Somerset border, Holcombe Rogus has a long history. Some of this is preserved in the church, where a set of records dates back to 1540. The 15th-century All Saints church and Church House are excellent examples of their kind.

HOLCOMBE ROGUS, FORD HOUSE c1960 H243047

Holcombe Rogus is a straggling village, and Ford House is slightly off the 'main' street. This view has its interest in the pack of hounds, possibly being exercised out of hunting season. If hunting is banned, these animals will be no more, joining tram drivers and lamplighters in the history books.

CULMSTOCK, MILLMOOR c1965 C312516

The crossing gate of the Culm Valley Railway hangs drunkenly after the closure of the line. This ran from Tiverton to Hemyock, and was a late (1876) arrival on the railway scene. The pub beyond still satisfies the needs of locals.

TIVERTON
Fore Street c1955 T55008
Tiverton's wealth was founded on wool and a school
which would become famous: Blundells. Later silk
would replace wool; today, light industry is where the
local wages are earned. It is still a prosperous little
town, and the view here has changed little over
the intervening years.

TIVERTON, BOLHAM WEIR AND THE FOOTBRIDGE c1955 T55018

The river Exe roars over Bolham Weir on its 55-mile journey from high on Exmoor in Somerset, down to the English Channel. Surprisingly, it rises quite close to the northern coast before journeying south. It is also an open-air supply line for water to Tiverton. A reservoir at Wimball always ensures a good supply of water to the river.

SAMPFORD PEVERELL, LOWER TOWN c1960 S355016

The somewhat shabby-looking Sampford Peverell of this photograph is much smarter today. Pubs and a superior restaurant have added a degree of cachet to this otherwise unremarkable village alongside the Grand Western Canal.

BICKLEIGH, THE FISHERMAN'S COT HOTEL AND THE RIVER EXE C1955 B84303
Today, you can still stay at the Fisherman's Cot hotel and try your luck in the river. The Exe was once a wonderful river for salmon; it was common for even the lowliest table to carry the fish. Today, it is much more rare, but sport is still possible. Trout and sea trout make up the rest of the catch.

CHERITON FITZPAINE, THE CHURCH c1960 C305005
The word 'Cheriton' was used in pre-Norman times, meaning 'churchtown', an indication of the village's antiquity.
The church is dedicated to St Matthew and is 15th-century. This rather scruffy-looking view is much tidied today.

BRAMPFORD SPEKE, THE POST OFFICE c1955 B385002
It is almost inevitable, but the village post office is no more. The door is infilled, and the building is now a house called Corner Cottage. For the visitor's delight, both buildings in this view retain their thatched roofs.

NEWTON ST CYRES, THE VILLAGE c1955 N83017
This is another unchanged view, a perfect example of the timelessness of this area. The buildings are better decorated, but the Shuttern Brook is still a ford.

UPTON HELLIONS, THE CHURCH c1965 U57035
This is really a parish with only the smallest hint of a hamlet attached. The tiny church has some Norman parts within its mainly 15th-century exterior. The road to the church finishes here: a complete dead end.

DOWN ST MARY, THE VILLAGE AND THE CHURCH c1960 D247004
A typical mid-Devon village, Down St Mary sits on the watershed dividing north and south Devon. Its open aspects make it a delightful place to live, especially with houses like this in view.

BOW, MAIN ROAD c1955 B834001
A straggling village lining the old Okehampton to Crediton road, Bow has a long history. It had a market charter by 1259 and an annual fair. This lasted until early in the last century. Relatively under-developed, there is still a sleepy feel to the village, despite the ever-present juggernauts roaring through.

BELSTONE, THE VILLAGE 1959 B296002
Ancient thatched cottages and narrow streets typify Belstone. This view is unchanged save for the removal of the pole carrying telephone wires.

OKEHAMPTON
Fore Street c1955 O12004
There are traffic problems in this view;
there is no change half a century later. The
chantry chapel of St James was built after
the town had moved away from the original
area, leaving All Saints church isolated.

OKEHAMPTON, FORE STREET c1965 O12045

A decade after photograph No O12004, the cars have changed. So too have the shop frontages, as they have yet again today. The garage on the left is replaced by a variety of shops, and the café on the right has become a leisure retailers.

OKEHAMPTON, FORE STREET c1955 O12030

We are looking the opposite way from photographs Nos O12004 and O12045. The town hall is on the right, followed by Market Street. Lloyds Bank is still there (with the initials TSB added to its title), whilst on the left The White Hart is unchanged, even to the beast on the roof of the canopy.

SOURTON, HIGHWAYMAN'S INN c1965 S766078

A lone Ford Cortina estate stands in the car park of this zany pub, not far from Okehampton. Today, the car park is full and the additions in the pub grounds have to be seen to be believed. There is an amazing childrens' play area, old barrels, a garden - in fact, almost everything you would not expect to find outside a pub. It is all great fun - and the additions keep coming.

DREWSTEIGNTON, THE CHURCH c1960 D85002

This is a small village on the northern slopes of Dartmoor, with Holy Trinity church at its centre. Built of Dartmoor granite in the early 16th century, the village has acquired a certain cachet today as an ideal place to live. But note the water pump in the left hand corner of the picture: not at all what today's 'townies' want, except as a garden ornament.

DREWSTEIGNTON, THE VILLAGE C 1960 D85005
Two boys seem to be squaring up to each other as the rest amuse themselves. The Old Inn is an attractive restaurant today, but not with Austin A30 saloons outside.

MORETONHAMPSTEAD, FINGLE BRIDGE c1960 M97023
Although listed as in Moretonhampstead, Fingle Bridge spans the river Teign just south of Drewsteignton. It is Elizabethan and, inevitably, built from granite. Then, as now, it is a tourist magnet.

CHAGFORD, THE SQUARE c1960 C559078

Time changes little. The Square is the centre of Chagford, and the Three Crowns Hotel (left) remains as rather a smart place to eat, drink or stay. The Ring o' Bells a little further along is still where it has been for years and, across the road, Lloyds Bank with the thatched roof still graces the area. Unlike their counterparts Barclays, Lloyds seem to have retained far more of their rural branches.

DUNSFORD, BRITTON STREET c1960 D118018

A tiny village on the eastern edge of Dartmoor and on the northern slopes of the river Teign, Dunsford has buildings with thatch and cob aplenty. The dominant position of St Mary's Church is clear from this view.

MORETONHAMPSTEAD, THE CHURCH c1960 M97018

Moretonhampstead is a charming market town nestling in a valley in the shade of eastern Dartmoor. A feature in the town is the church with its granite tower. Its exact age is uncertain, but the tower was under construction in 1418.

MANATON, THE MOOR c1955 M20016

This is a fine view of the eastern slopes of Dartmoor as seen from the village of Manaton. The Kestor Inn (as it is now known) is still a fine pub. Note the milk churns (centre). Today, milk is collected from farms by bulk tanker. In those days, the farmer brought his milk to a convenient point in churns. The dairy lorry then collected them from that point.

MANATON, FORGE CORNER c1960 M20017

Several symbols of the days when this picture was taken are clear here: there is no-where for pedestrians to walk, the road signs are small and easily missed, and there is a lack of cars. The Standard Vanguard was quite old when this photograph was taken. They were originally introduced not long after the war.

LUSTLEIGH, THE CHURCH c1955 L115046

St John the Baptist's church in Lustleigh is a complicated building by the standards of other Moors churches. Some of it actually dates back to Norman times, but the bulk is 15th-century. When this picture was taken, the interior was lit by candle and paraffin lamp.

LUSTLEIGH
Primrose Cottage c1965
For centuries Lustleigh was a remote village. Then it was 'discovered'; and incomers started to build. They created monstrosities that purported to follow the existing style. They failed. Fortunately, there are still enough originals - such as can be seen in this picture - to retain most of the atmosphere of this special area.

◆

BOVEY TRACEY
Fore Street c1965
Narrow streets are still a feature of Bovey Tracey. Note the car on the left. Again, we have a car registered in 1966 (in the Newcastle-on-Tyne area), allowing the picture to be dated a little more accurately.

LUSTLEIGH, PRIMROSE COTTAGE c1965 L115062

BOVEY TRACEY, FORE STREET c1965 B161042

BOVEY TRACEY, THE PARISH CHURCH c1955 B161008

Here we see the 14th-century tower of the church of St Peter, St Paul and St Thomas of Canterbury. It was built to replace an earlier church that had burnt down. That one was constructed by Sir William de Tracy, one of the men involved in the murder of Thomas à Beckett in 1170. This was his penance for that act.

ILSINGTON, THE VILLAGE AND THE CHURCH c1965 I8009
This is an unusual village in that although most of the housing stock is ancient, much renovation has taken place. Once, the local authority decided to condemn them as insanitary. This created uproar, and peace was only restored when the council agreed to modernisation. Smart and spruce, the village today is a picture.

ILSINGTON, THE POST OFFICE c1965 I8010
Overall, Devon has done rather well in their retention of sub-post offices. Ilsington is a case in point. Up-country, villages much bigger than this have lost their post offices.

HAYTOR VALE c1960 H56002
Haytor Vale is in an area of intense quarrying, where Dartmoor granite was won. There was an extensive tramway system in the quarries which enabled the large lumps of stone to be carried down to the coast for shipping around the country. The Rock Inn still exists in the village, a popular haunt for holidaymakers and locals alike. The car in centre shot is a taxi.

WIDECOMBE IN THE MOOR, THE VILLAGE c1955 W95029
This is the village made famous by the eponymous song. The 'grey mare' referred to in the song indicates a horsey scenario, and Widecombe Fair was a place where Dartmoor ponies were sold. The Old Inn in the picture still exists.

HEXWORTHY, THE FOREST INN c1955 H240001

Hexworthy
The Forest Inn c1955
You will be hard-pressed to spot the difference between this view and the one to be seen today. There are a few more cars, the trees have grown, but otherwise this free house serving excellent food is pretty much as it is here.

Dartmeet c1960
This is where the east and west Dart rivers meet. It has been a popular visitor location for years now, as witnessed by the collection of coaches - far outnumbering private cars. Today, the area is surfaced and parking is much more formally arranged.

DARTMEET c1960 D5007

DARTMEET, THE RIVER DART AND THE CLAPPER BRIDGE c1965 D5026
Taken from the road bridge, this delightful view of what is left of the old clapper bridge at Dartmeet is redolent of an earlier age. Water continues to hold a fascination for young and old alike.

TWO BRIDGES, THE HOTEL c1960 T153006
This 18th-century old coaching inn is as popular with visitors today as it has always been. Indeed, it has been extended since this view was taken: the area to the right of the main building has been replaced with further rooms and an attractive clock tower on top. The pub serves its own brew.

TWO BRIDGES, THE TWO BRIDGES c1960 T153010

TWO BRIDGES
The Two Bridges c1960
Here we see the West Dart River at Two Bridges. This, the older bridge of the two, offers gorgeous reflections in the water. The newer road bridge can be seen beyond the arches. The pub is to the right of this shot.

◆

POSTBRIDGE
The Old Clapper Bridge c1955
1,100ft above sea level, this bridge is reputed to be one of the oldest of its kind in the country, set in an area of great antiquity. All around, there is evidence of prehistoric man having lived up here. Today, a few cottages scattered around a pub is the sum total of human activity.

POSTBRIDGE, THE OLD CLAPPER BRIDGE c1955 P102004

PRINCETOWN, THE SQUARE C1955 P115001
Princetown, the location of Dartmoor prison, is in a bleak, inhospitable part of the Moor. Despite that, the town - never to be described as beautiful- has a certain something that makes it attractive. Ponies wander freely around the street, much to the joy of visitors.

PRINCETOWN, DARTMOOR PONIES c1965 P115024
It is a decade after view no P115001, and the Railway Hotel has become the Devils Elbow and ponies still roam. Today, the pub has reverted (almost) to its old name: it is now the Station Inn. The grocers on the left hand corner is no more: it is now The Sherlock Homes Experience. The ponies are walking over what is now a mini-roundabout.

YELVERTON, DARTMOOR PONIES c1955 Y10014
We are on the edge of Dartmoor at Yelverton, and this pony seems to have made a conquest. What visitors to the area never realise is that these are wild animals which will nip you as soon as look at you, especially if there is no food in the proffered hand.

DAWLISH, LADY'S MILE FARM CAMPING SITE c1960 D12117
This view shows holidaymaking in Devon 40 years ago. There will have been some epic journeys to reach this site. Around this time, before the motorways were built, the road system was under as much pressure as it is today. Journey times were judged on how long it took to negotiate the Exeter by-pass: hours every weekend.

DAWLISH, LADY'S MILE FARM SHOP AND CAMPING SITE c1960 D12119

TEIGNMOUTH, NORTH BEACH c1960 T21064

DAWLISH
Lady's Mile Farm Shop and Camping Site c1960

This site was opened in 1952 when the owner decided to get out of pig farming. It still exists today, although most visitors now have a caravan. There is no queuing at the house for a pint of milk either: a purpose-built shop is now provided - along with two swimming pools, an adventure playground, a nine-hole golf course, laundrettes and a games room. The old house still stands.

◆

TEIGNMOUTH
North Beach c1960

Taken from the pier, this view of the beach also shows the town off to its best advantage. The industrial end of the town, including the port, are behind the cameraman.

TEIGNMOUTH, THE PROMENADE c1955 T21011

Towards the eastern end of the town is a delightful walk alongside the sea towards Dawlish; the man in the centre of the picture appears to be ready to tackle it. The church is St Michael's, and the spindly legs of the pier are plain to see.

SHALDON, FROM TEIGNMOUTH POINT c1955 S100010

This is the Teign estuary, a narrow strip of water with Teignmouth behind and Shaldon ahead. The moving boat is the small passenger ferry between the two places. The water here is surprisingly deep, allowing ships of some considerable size to tie up at the quay out of sight to the right.

SHALDON, NESS HOUSE c1955 S100038
We are looking out to sea with the river Teign on the extreme left. This is a delightful area in which to relax. Ness House is a rather attractive hotel which has a Les Routiers listing, and has changed little since this view was taken.

SHALDON, FORE STREET c1965 S100051
A real holiday shop on the left indicates that this is prime holidaymakers' territory. Shaldon, though, is not blessed with beaches, facing as it does to the river Teign. A trip across to Teignmouth soon solves that problem. The Clifford Arms on the left and Lloyds Bank on the right are both still operating in the town.

MAIDENCOMBE, BUNGALOW TEA GARDENS C1955 M167017

Thatch is still prevalent in the Torbay area, and this house, with its corrugated-iron business attached, is typical of so much here. Even the tea gardens is typical. This sort of establishment was ubiquitous at the time of this picture. Today, they are almost an endangered species.

MAIDENCOMBE, THE MAIN ROAD C1955 M167024

This is a sight almost unknown today: just one vehicle on the move in the village. Today, it is a constant battle to get anywhere and, having eventually made it, to find space to park.

MAIDENCOMBE, THE BEACH c1955 M167039
What passes for the beach at Maidencombe is packed with holidaymakers. Note that the lady swimmers are wearing caps. With few expensive perms to protect, today's bathers generally swim without.

ODDICOMBE, THE BEACH c1960 O59038
Oddicombe Beach in Torquay is still served by a cliff railway, as can be seen to the left of this view. That there is more sand to go to is clear from the serried ranks of deck chairs in place on the beach.

TORQUAY, THE HARBOUR c1965 T62593
We are in Torbay proper now. This stretches from a promontory within the town known as Hope's Nose south to Berry Head in Brixham. The harbour is a popular yacht haven (as is clear) and the acres of new building that has taken place since the war can be seen behind, some of it still under construction at the time of this view.

COCKINGTON, THE FORGE c1950 C134090

This is a village of exquisite beauty with acres of thatch drawing visitors from far and near. It is actually a suburb of Torquay now, but you would never realise it, so well has its old-world atmosphere been retained.

MARLDON, THE CHURCH c1965 M168003

This village has managed (just) to retain its individual identity amid the Torquay/Paignton sprawl. It is set on a hill, and much of the old has disappeared, replaced by more modern buildings. But the place still seems to exude a feeling of individuality. Is it the church that does it? St John the Baptist's church is 15th-century, and is quite large for the size of the village.

GOODRINGTON, THE BEACH c1965 G32011

Goodrington Sands are famous in this area as the best around. The people in this view seem to be relaxing and enjoying themselves in their (now almost extinct) deck chairs. The land mass in the view is Roundham Head, with Paignton beyond.

GOODRINGTON, THE CHILDREN'S SAILING POOL c1965 G32056

We are still in an age of relative innocence as lots of model yachts vie for any available wind. The youngster of today would need a radio control box with electrically-driven boats before showing much interest.

BRIXHAM
The Harbour c1950 B214022
A charming small town clustered around the harbour, Brixham has long earned its living from the sea.
Here, a variety of fishing boats mix with some early pleasure boats and even a few yachts.

BRIXHAM, THE JETTY c1955 B214107

GALMPTON, THE VILLAGE c1965 G134004

BRIXHAM
The Jetty c1955

Before the war, Brixham was the leading fishing port in Devon. At one time, there were almost 300 trawlers employing 1600 seamen. Hundreds more people on shore built and repaired the ships and manufactured sails and clothing, whilst the women knitted underwear, packed the fish and made nets. The EC has utterly ruined the port.

◆

GALMPTON
The Village c1965

Galmpton is old: it was mentioned in Domesday. Today it has lost much of its identity as development from Goodrington has encroached. On the left-hand side of the road is an old sign indicating a school, a relic of the past.

KINGSWEAR, GENERAL VIEW C1960 K34001

KINGSWEAR
General View c1960
Photographed from the Dartmouth side of the Dart river, Kingswear was the railhead for that town; passengers crossed the estuary on a ferry. Now that railway has closed as part of the main line, and is steam-operated privately. Wagons and carriages can be seen behind the trip boat.

◆

KINGSWEAR
The Backwaters c1960
This view of Kingswear is from upstream, beyond the area generally known as Dartmouth Harbour. Smoke from the left-hand shore again indicates railway activity.

KINGSWEAR, THE BACKWATERS C1960 K34003

STOKE GABRIEL, THE CHURCH HOUSE INN c1960 S366028

STOKE GABRIEL
The Church House Inn c1960

On a creek just off the river Dart, Stoke Gabriel is a place of narrow streets and surprising vistas: each corner reveals new interest. The village bobby (come back please, all is forgiven) is keeping a weather eye on our photographer. He has gone, but the pub and post office have lasted.

◆

STOKE GABRIEL
The Victoria and Albert Inn c1960

Here we have a delightful view of the Albert and Victoria Inn at Stoke Gabriel. Yes, you can eat, drink and be merry there to this day, but Tivvy Ales belong to the history books. The quality of their ales would have today's CAMRA people salivating at the prospect. The brewery - in Tiverton - closed in 1965.

STOKE GABRIEL, THE VICTORIA AND ALBERT INN c1960 S366045

STOKE GABRIEL, THE CREEK c1965 S366049
Needless to say, the church here is dedicated to St Gabriel. Much of it has been rebuilt over the years, but the tower dates back to the 13th century.

TOTNES, THE BRIDGE c1965 T66105
For many years, this was the only way to cross the river Dart in Totnes. This particular work was executed by Charles Fowler, a local architect in 1828. In more recent times, a further bridge was built to relieve the pressure of traffic in the town centre.

TOTNES
The Dartmouth Boat c1965 T66079
The paddle steamer 'Kingswear Castle' is leaving the
Steamer Quay in Totnes, bound for Dartmouth. Built in
1924, she worked the river for 40 years before being
withdrawn. Rescued by a preservation group, this venerable
steamer is now based in Chatham (Kent) where she still
cruises up and down a river: this time the Medway.

TOTNES, THE EAST GATE c1965 T66117
Totnes became a walled town in about 1215. Although much has now disappeared, the East Gate (rebuilt in the early 1500s) in Fore Street still exists. Examples of some of the other fine buildings in this town can be seen alongside the gate.

NEWTON ABBOTT, ST LEONARD'S CLOCK TOWER C1950 N32005
St Leonard's Tower is all that remains of a 14th-century church, demolished in 1836. Much road widening has been carried out in this area, all to accommodate the tower.

NEWTON ABBOTT
Queen Street c1955 N32035
The town only developed when railways arrived in the area. It formed a natural junction for the Torbay area with the Exeter to Cornwall line. There was also a branch to Moretonhampstead. Thus, there are few really old buildings in town, but Victorian shopping fronts still abound. This view is typical of the time.

BUCKFASTLEIGH, BUCKFAST ABBEY c1955 B238030

This abbey was founded in around 1030 by King Canute. It fell out of use for a time in the early 11th century, but was re-founded and occupied by Cistercian monks from then until the Reformation. The abbey church is a remarkable reconstruction. Just over a century ago, a band of Benedictine monks bought the remains of the old abbey and laboured for forty years to re-create what we see today.

BUCKFASTLEIGH, FORE STREET c1965 B238061

This is the narrow main street in Buckfastleigh. The sun blind on the left overhangs the road, and must have been a target for any passing pantechnicon. On the right is another Lloyds Bank, still open to this day.

PLYMOUTH, THE BATHING POOL FROM THE LIGHTHOUSE c1950 P60019
Plymouth is not normally thought of as a seaside town, but many people take their holidays in the city to this day. If the swimming pools on the cliff edge have fallen into disuse, there are many superb suntraps on the cliffs overlooking the Sound.

PLYMOUTH, THE CLIFFS c1965 P60075
Beneath Plymouth Hoe is the most popular area for visitors, as can be seen from this view. To the right - with the flagpole - is the Royal Citadel. Henry VIII had authorised defensive works to be carried out on this site overlooking the Sound, although the present fort dates back to 1670

PLYMPTON, THE GUILDHALL c1955 P61029

This fine civic building dates from 1696. Little has changed here on Fore Street. Plympton Earl (or Plympton St Maurice as it is also known) was the birthplace of Sir Joshua Reynolds, the great English painter.

NEWTON FERRERS, NEWTON HILL c1965 N33116

As you descend a steep hill towards the slipway, you will find that this view is virtually unchanged today. The shop on the right has become more specialised, offering hot home-baked bread, fish, pies, pasties and cakes.

NOSS MAYO, THE WATERSIDE C1950 N49054
On either side of a creek off the Yealm estuary sit Newton Ferrers and Noss Mayo. Creels and small boats are the clue to what maintained Noss Mayo before yachtsmen found it as a delightful and sheltered harbour.

NOSS MAYO, THE VILLAGE FROM NEWTON FERRERS c1965 N49041
At the bottom of the hill seen in photograph No N33116 is a slipway. This looks across to Noss Mayo and St Peter's church, built in 1882. This replaced an earlier one, built to the south on the cliffs at Stoke and far away from any housing, probably to serve as a landmark for sailors on this treacherous coast.

NEWTON FERRERS, THE VIEW FROM NOSS MAYO c1965 N33104
Looking across the water towards Newton Ferrers gives a clear indication of how the village clings to the side of a hill. Bad roads from the Plymouth area have, to some degree, sheltered the village from becoming a dormitory to the city.

MODBURY, BROAD STREET c1955 M172013
Looking west, this view has changed little in the intervening half century. The large Co-op on the right still trades as does (inevitably) Lloyds Bank on the right. It is remarkable how this particular bank appears in so many photographs to the virtual exclusion of the other High Street names. Could our photographer have had shares in the company?

MODBURY, CHURCH STREET c1955 M172014
A little further along from photograph No M172013, this scene was recorded. The pub on the right still trades, but the traffic along this road is now quite horrendous.

RINGMORE, THE JOURNEY'S END INN c1955 R258013

This is a gorgeous village with plenty of thatch. It also has impossibly narrow streets and absolutely no-where to park. If you decide to visit, park at the top, on the edge, and walk. You will find this view unchanged save for the removal of the white posts outside the pub.

RINGMORE, THE VILLAGE c1955 R258002

Here we see an example of the state of the roads in Ringmore. They have changed little since this view was taken. The properties have been smartened up somewhat, but the general impression that this place just happened rather than was planned still pervades.

LODDISWELL, THE VILLAGE c1960 L531011

Much of this place remains as it was when the photographer visited. The small shed (centre) with the sagging roof has gone, and Hillside Cottage next door has extended into that space. East View(left) is unchanged.

BANTHAM, THE VILLAGE FROM HAM GATE c1955 B16012

This tiny settlement - it can scarcely even qualify as being a hamlet - lies at the mouth of the river Avon on the western bank. These visiting cars will have negotiated a typically narrow Devonian lane for several miles to reach this spot.

BANTHAM, THE BOATHOUSE AND THE RIVER c1955 B16001
This is a most delightful structure, and the thatch is in perfect repair. Being so far removed from the beaten track, places like this could be built for practical use and last for years before some visitor would fall in love with it and decide to make it a home.

BANTHAM, HAM FROM SANDHILLS c1955 B16019
It does not take much exploration of this pretty corner to locate these few buildings. After all, there is little else to be seen. Because of the total lack of railways earlier and of roads today, this corner remained untouched by tourism until relatively recent times.

THURLESTONE, VIEW FROM THE LINKS HOTEL c1950 T42013

Less than a mile from Bantham, this village has developed to a degree. The village is built on rising ground, and this somewhat marshy area is to the south. The slender church tower belongs to All Saints, and was built in the 15th century.

THURLESTONE, THE VILLAGE c1940 T42027

A wonderfully evocative view of Thurlestone during the early days of the last war. The small cart to the left appears to be horse-drawn, and could well be selling fish. The general smartening-up of these villages that would follow the war is clearly already needed here.

THURLESTONE, THE VILLAGE c1950 T42015

This view was taken a decade after photograph No T42027 and in the same spot. Although the retailer's vehicle is now powered by the internal combustion engine, there is ample evidence of the proximity of horse-power : look at the road surface. Thurlestone remains a village of peace and beauty.

SALCOMBE, VIEW FROM SNAPES POINT C1955 S44057
A small town at the mouth of the Kingsbridge estuary, Salcombe is mainly a yachting centre today. This vantage point - beyond the town - offers the perfect view of the landing stage, left of the houses and out to sea.

SALCOMBE, FROM EAST PORTLEMOUTH c1965 S44270
This view of Salcombe was taken from the east side of the estuary. It is a decade after photograph No 44057, and already the accumulation of boats can be seen. This place, in common with other coastal parts of the South Hams, never suffered from mass tourism because of the absence of a railway, although there was a line to Kingsbridge which opened in 1893. This provided a rapid increase in visitor numbers.

KINGSBRIDGE, THE SHAMBLES c1960 K25040
The Shambles is an old shopping area of the town in Fore Street; these units are still in use, and have been smartened considerably by the application of white paint to the masonry. To the right, the Kings Arms pub has also been painted - in pink and white.

KINGSBRIDGE, THE PS 'COMPTON CASTLE', SQUARE QUAY c1960 K25068

This is a sister ship to the 'Kingswear Castle', which we encountered in Totnes in Chapter 3. This, too, was employed in the leisure trade, offering holidaymakers the chance of a quick sea cruise. The quayside now has small craft and yachts moored alongside.

STOKENHAM, THE CHURCH c1960 S197046

St Michael and All Angels was built around the 15th century with a tower, a style quite common in this part of Devon. The Church House Inn still stands alongside, selling refreshments to thirsty visitors.

TORCROSS
The Square c1960 T61039
Torcross is a small settlement on the sweeping sandy area
that is Start Bay. Catering for visitors today, it was once
famed for its crabs, which were sold in London to great
acclaim. Much of what can be seen here still remains.

STOKENHAM, START POINT LIGHTHOUSE c1955 S197001
Start Point is the southern headland, and has been guarded by a lighthouse here since 1836. In common with all lighthouses today, it is operated automatically, and the keeper belongs to history.

TORCROSS, THE BEACH AND SLAPTON LEY c1965 T61049
Just south of Torcross is a low cliff which served as a vantage point for this picture. US forces used this area to practice their D-Day landings in Normandy. There were accidents too, resulting in loss of life. Today, a memorial can be seen further along the beach. Note, behind the houses, an expanse of water. This will be seen more clearly in photograph No S140004.

SLAPTON, THE LEY c1960 S140004
Two miles long and up to half a mile wide, Slapton Ley is fresh water, despite being separated from the ocean by a narrow spit of land. This is now a nature reserve, and has many fascinating birds to see.

SLAPTON, THE VILLAGE c1960 S140021
It is milking time: the cows return to the farmyard, and a tractor (extreme right) makes sure the beasts go in the direction they should. The 14th-century church is dedicated to St James the Greater.

STOKE FLEMING, THE VILLAGE c1965 S200035
Another Devon village with narrow streets, Stoke Fleming sits high atop the cliffs above Start Bay. The Meadow Dairy used to be a chain of grocers, long before supermarkets made any impression in this country. They, too, are now consigned to the history book.

STOKE FLEMING, THE ENDSLEIGH HOTEL c1965 S200040
Still to be found on New Road in Stoke, the Endsleigh Hotel maintains a fine tradition of Devonian hospitality. Many other similar establishments have closed in recent years as the British holidaymaker heads for more exotic destinations.

DARTMOUTH, THE FLOATING BRIDGE C1955 D7010
This is one of the old ferries that brought cars across the Teign from Kingswear. The date that this service was established has never been satisfactorily decided. Suffice it to say that it has existed for many centuries.

DARTMOUTH
The Inner Harbour c1955 D7087

Here we have a lovely view of a lovely town. Development in Dartmouth has been severely constricted by the steep terrain, and this has contributed greatly to the preservation of the town; the 'developers' of the post war period were not able to despoil it.

HARBERTONFORD, THE BRIDGE c1960 H494009
The Harbourne river rises on Dartmoor and empties into the Teign not far beyond Harbertonford. By its very name, it is clear that there was a ford here in years gone by. The water was first bridged in the late 16th century. The large house (centre) is called Ford House, and the white building to the right is the Hungry Horse Restaurant.

HARBERTONFORD, OLD ROAD AND THE BRIDGE c1965 H494015
The speed restriction posts have gone, but the shop and post office to the right still exist. The end building is The Maltster's Arms.

IVYBRIDGE, FORE STREET c1955 122016
For many years, Ivybridge suffered a ceaseless pounding from traffic. The A38 was the main road from Exeter and beyond to Plymouth. Now a by-pass is in place, and the town is the happier for it. The vehicle on the left is a corporation dust cart with a trailer on the back. This was used to collect waste paper: an example of re-cycling half a century ago. There really is nothing new under the sun.

IVYBRIDGE, THE BRIDGE c1955 122043
The river Erme tumbles through, and a prettier scene of rural England would be hard to find.

MILTON COMBE, THE WHO'D HAVE THOUGHT IT c1955 M170014

Before it became a desirable place to live, Milton Combe looked somewhat run-down. Now all the walls are whitewashed, and the place looks a treat. The pub still has the same delightful name, and has existed since the 16th century. It was named thus because, when the owner applied for a licence, no-one expected him to get it. When he did, what started as an opinion became a name.

MILTON COMBE, BROOKSIDE STORES c1955 M170015

With a new roof, this building still exists, but not as a retail establishment: it is now The Old Post House. The wall to the left belonged to the pub, and was knocked down to form the entrance to a car park.

MILTON COMBE, THE VILLAGE c1955 M170016
We are now further into the village, and it is difficult to find any changes since the cameraman visited half a century ago. Perhaps the tractor has gone though. It is still gorgeous, unspoilt and a delightful place to visit.

LYDFORD, THE CASTLE INN c1955 L119004
In this view, Lydford looked rather bleak. That was before the tourists started arriving en masse. Now it is delightfully pretty, bordering on the twee. The pub has clematis and wisteria climbing the walls, and the electricity poles have disappeared.

TAVISTOCK
Duke Street c1955 T17043
There have been many changes here. The Newmarket Hotel is a Lloyds Bank branch, the National Provincial has gone, and so has the Methodist church complete with its steeple.

BEDFORD SQ

TAVISTOCK, THE BRIDGE AND THE WEIR c1955 T17056
Abbey Bridge has changed little. The trees to be seen here are much bigger now, and the walk alongside the Tavy is even more popular. This is a quite delightful area.

TAVISTOCK, THE GUILDHALL SQUARE c1955 T17099
The Guildhall was built in 1848 and with the war memorial is in Bedford Square. The weird vehicle left of centre appears to be an early motor caravan. And it appears to be just that: a caravan body joined onto a chassis of some kind.

Index

Axminster 16-17, 18

Bantham 93, 94

Belstone 47

Beer 34

Bickleigh 43

Bovey Tracey 56, 57

Bow 47

Brampford Speke 45

Branscombe 35

Brixham 74-75, 76

Buckfastleigh 86

Budleigh Salterton 31

Chagford 53

Cheriton Fitzpaine 44

Cockington 72

Colyton 35, 36

Culmstock 39

Dartmeet 60, 61

Dartmouth 105, 106-107

Dawlish 65, 66

Down St Mary 46

Drewsteignton 51, 52

Dunsford 53

Exeter 26, 27, 28

Exmouth 29

Galmpton 76

Gittisham 21

Goodrington 73

Harbertonford 108

Haytor Vale 59

Hexworthy 60

Holcombe Rogus 38, 39

Honiton 20

Ilsington 58

Ivybridge 109

Kilmington 37, 38

Kingsbridge 98, 99

Kingswear 77

Littleham 30

Loddiswell 93

Lustleigh 55, 56

Lydford 111

Maidencombe 69, 70

Manaton 54, 55

Marldon 72

Membury 18

Milton Combe 110, 111

Modbury 91

Moretonhampstead 52, 54

Newton Abbott 83, 84-85

Newton Ferrers 88, 90

Newton Poppleford 32

Newton St Cyres 45

Noss Mayo 89, 90

Oddicombe 71

Offwell 19

Okehampton 48-49, 50

Otterton 31

Ottery St Mary 21, 22-23

Plymouth 87

Plympton 88

Postbridge 62

Princetown 63, 64

Ringmore 92

Rockbeare 24

Salcombe 97, 98

Sampford 42

Shaldon 67, 68

Shute 37

Sidmouth 33

Slapton 103

Sourton 51

Stokenham 99, 102

Stoke Flemming 104

Stoke Gabriel 78, 79

Tavistock 112-113, 114

Teignmouth 66, 67

Thurleston 95, 96

Tiverton 40-41, 42

Topsham 28

Torcross 100-101, 102

Torquay 71

Totnes 79, 80-81, 82

Two Bridges 61, 62

Upton Hellions 46

Widecombe in the Moor 59

Woodbury 24, 25

Yarcombe 19

Yelverton 64

Frith Book Co Titles

www.francisfrith.co.uk

The Frith Book Company publishes over 100 new titles each year. A selection of those currently available are listed below. For latest catalogue please contact Frith Book Co.

Town Books 96 pages, approx 100 photos. County and Themed Books 128 pages, approx 150 photos (unless specified). All titles hardback laminated case and jacket except those indicated pb (paperback)

Title	ISBN	Price	Title	ISBN	Price
Amersham, Chesham & Rickmansworth (pb)			Derby (pb)	1-85937-367-4	£9.99
	1-85937-340-2	£9.99	Derbyshire (pb)	1-85937-196-5	£9.99
Ancient Monuments & Stone Circles	1-85937-143-4	£17.99	Devon (pb)	1-85937-297-x	£9.99
Aylesbury (pb)	1-85937-227-9	£9.99	Dorset (pb)	1-85937-269-4	£9.99
Bakewell	1-85937-113-2	£12.99	Dorset Churches	1-85937-172-8	£17.99
Barnstaple (pb)	1-85937-300-3	£9.99	Dorset Coast (pb)	1-85937-299-6	£9.99
Bath (pb)	1-85937419-0	£9.99	Dorset Living Memories	1-85937-210-4	£14.99
Bedford (pb)	1-85937-205-8	£9.99	Down the Severn	1-85937-118-3	£14.99
Berkshire (pb)	1-85937-191-4	£9.99	Down the Thames (pb)	1-85937-278-3	£9.99
Berkshire Churches	1-85937-170-1	£17.99	Down the Trent	1-85937-311-9	£14.99
Blackpool (pb)	1-85937-382-8	£9.99	Dublin (pb)	1-85937-231-7	£9.99
Bognor Regis (pb)	1-85937-431-x	£9.99	East Anglia (pb)	1-85937-265-1	£9.99
Bournemouth	1-85937-067-5	£12.99	East London	1-85937-080-2	£14.99
Bradford (pb)	1-85937-204-x	£9.99	East Sussex	1-85937-130-2	£14.99
Brighton & Hove(pb)	1-85937-192-2	£8.99	Eastbourne	1-85937-061-6	£12.99
Bristol (pb)	1-85937-264-3	£9.99	Edinburgh (pb)	1-85937-193-0	£8.99
British Life A Century Ago (pb)	1-85937-213-9	£9.99	England in the 1880s	1-85937-331-3	£17.99
Buckinghamshire (pb)	1-85937-200-7	£9.99	English Castles (pb)	1-85937-434-4	£9.99
Camberley (pb)	1-85937-222-8	£9.99	English Country Houses	1-85937-161-2	£17.99
Cambridge (pb)	1-85937-422-0	£9.99	Essex (pb)	1-85937-270-8	£9.99
Cambridgeshire (pb)	1-85937-420-4	£9.99	Exeter	1-85937-126-4	£12.99
Canals & Waterways (pb)	1-85937-291-0	£9.99	Exmoor	1-85937-132-9	£14.99
Canterbury Cathedral (pb)	1-85937-179-5	£9.99	Falmouth	1-85937-066-7	£12.99
Cardiff (pb)	1-85937-093-4	£9.99	Folkestone (pb)	1-85937-124-8	£9.99
Carmarthenshire	1-85937-216-3	£14.99	Glasgow (pb)	1-85937-190-6	£9.99
Chelmsford (pb)	1-85937-310-0	£9.99	Gloucestershire	1-85937-102-7	£14.99
Cheltenham (pb)	1-85937-095-0	£9.99	Great Yarmouth (pb)	1-85937-426-3	£9.99
Cheshire (pb)	1-85937-271-6	£9.99	Greater Manchester (pb)	1-85937-266-x	£9.99
Chester	1-85937-090-x	£12.99	Guildford (pb)	1-85937-410-7	£9.99
Chesterfield	1-85937-378-x	£9.99	Hampshire (pb)	1-85937-279-1	£9.99
Chichester (pb)	1-85937-228-7	£9.99	Hampshire Churches (pb)	1-85937-207-4	£9.99
Colchester (pb)	1-85937-188-4	£8.99	Harrogate	1-85937-423-9	£9.99
Cornish Coast	1-85937-163-9	£14.99	Hastings & Bexhill (pb)	1-85937-131-0	£9.99
Cornwall (pb)	1-85937-229-5	£9.99	Heart of Lancashire (pb)	1-85937-197-3	£9.99
Cornwall Living Memories	1-85937-248-1	£14.99	Helston (pb)	1-85937-214-7	£9.99
Cotswolds (pb)	1-85937-230-9	£9.99	Hereford (pb)	1-85937-175-2	£9.99
Cotswolds Living Memories	1-85937-255-4	£14.99	Herefordshire	1-85937-174-4	£14.99
County Durham	1-85937-123-x	£14.99	Hertfordshire (pb)	1-85937-247-3	£9.99
Croydon Living Memories	1-85937-162-0	£9.99	Horsham (pb)	1-85937-432-8	£9.99
Cumbria	1-85937-101-9	£14.99	Humberside	1-85937-215-5	£14.99
Dartmoor	1-85937-145-0	£14.99	Hythe, Romney Marsh & Ashford	1-85937-256-2	£9.99

Available from your local bookshop or from the publisher

Frith Book Co Titles (continued)

Ipswich (pb)	1-85937-424-7	£9.99	St Ives (pb)	1-85937415-8	£9.99
Ireland (pb)	1-85937-181-7	£9.99	Scotland (pb)	1-85937-182-5	£9.99
Isle of Man (pb)	1-85937-268-6	£9.99	Scottish Castles (pb)	1-85937-323-2	£9.99
Isles of Scilly	1-85937-136-1	£14.99	Sevenoaks & Tunbridge	1-85937-057-8	£12.99
Isle of Wight (pb)	1-85937-429-8	£9.99	Sheffield, South Yorks (pb)	1-85937-267-8	£9.99
Isle of Wight Living Memories	1-85937-304-6	£14.99	Shrewsbury (pb)	1-85937-325-9	£9.99
Kent (pb)	1-85937-189-2	£9.99	Shropshire (pb)	1-85937-326-7	£9.99
Kent Living Memories	1-85937-125-6	£14.99	Somerset	1-85937-153-1	£14.99
Lake District (pb)	1-85937-275-9	£9.99	South Devon Coast	1-85937-107-8	£14.99
Lancaster, Morecambe & Heysham (pb)	1-85937-233-3	£9.99	South Devon Living Memories	1-85937-168-x	£14.99
Leeds (pb)	1-85937-202-3	£9.99	South Hams	1-85937-220-1	£14.99
Leicester	1-85937-073-x	£12.99	Southampton (pb)	1-85937-427-1	£9.99
Leicestershire (pb)	1-85937-185-x	£9.99	Southport (pb)	1-85937-425-5	£9.99
Lincolnshire (pb)	1-85937-433-6	£9.99	Staffordshire	1-85937-047-0	£12.99
Liverpool & Merseyside (pb)	1-85937-234-1	£9.99	Stratford upon Avon	1-85937-098-5	£12.99
London (pb)	1-85937-183-3	£9.99	Suffolk (pb)	1-85937-221-x	£9.99
Ludlow (pb)	1-85937-176-0	£9.99	Suffolk Coast	1-85937-259-7	£14.99
Luton (pb)	1-85937-235-x	£9.99	Surrey (pb)	1-85937-240-6	£9.99
Maidstone	1-85937-056-x	£14.99	Sussex (pb)	1-85937-184-1	£9.99
Manchester (pb)	1-85937-198-1	£9.99	Swansea (pb)	1-85937-167-1	£9.99
Middlesex	1-85937-158-2	£14.99	Tees Valley & Cleveland	1-85937-211-2	£14.99
New Forest	1-85937-128-0	£14.99	Thanet (pb)	1-85937-116-7	£9.99
Newark (pb)	1-85937-366-6	£9.99	Tiverton (pb)	1-85937-178-7	£9.99
Newport, Wales (pb)	1-85937-258-9	£9.99	Torbay	1-85937-063-2	£12.99
Newquay (pb)	1-85937-421-2	£9.99	Truro	1-85937-147-7	£12.99
Norfolk (pb)	1-85937-195-7	£9.99	Victorian and Edwardian Cornwall	1-85937-252-x	£14.99
Norfolk Living Memories	1-85937-217-1	£14.99	Victorian & Edwardian Devon	1-85937-253-8	£14.99
Northamptonshire	1-85937-150-7	£14.99	Victorian & Edwardian Kent	1-85937-149-3	£14.99
Northumberland Tyne & Wear (pb)	1-85937-281-3	£9.99	Vic & Ed Maritime Album	1-85937-144-2	£17.99
North Devon Coast	1-85937-146-9	£14.99	Victorian and Edwardian Sussex	1-85937-157-4	£14.99
North Devon Living Memories	1-85937-261-9	£14.99	Victorian & Edwardian Yorkshire	1-85937-154-x	£14.99
North London	1-85937-206-6	£14.99	Victorian Seaside	1-85937-159-0	£17.99
North Wales (pb)	1-85937-298-8	£9.99	Villages of Devon (pb)	1-85937-293-7	£9.99
North Yorkshire (pb)	1-85937-236-8	£9.99	Villages of Kent (pb)	1-85937-294-5	£9.99
Norwich (pb)	1-85937-194-9	£8.99	Villages of Sussex (pb)	1-85937-295-3	£9.99
Nottingham (pb)	1-85937-324-0	£9.99	Warwickshire (pb)	1-85937-203-1	£9.99
Nottinghamshire (pb)	1-85937-187-6	£9.99	Welsh Castles (pb)	1-85937-322-4	£9.99
Oxford (pb)	1-85937-411-5	£9.99	West Midlands (pb)	1-85937-289-9	£9.99
Oxfordshire (pb)	1-85937-430-1	£9.99	West Sussex	1-85937-148-5	£14.99
Peak District (pb)	1-85937-280-5	£9.99	West Yorkshire (pb)	1-85937-201-5	£9.99
Penzance	1-85937-069-1	£12.99	Weymouth (pb)	1-85937-209-0	£9.99
Peterborough (pb)	1-85937-219-8	£9.99	Wiltshire (pb)	1-85937-277-5	£9.99
Piers	1-85937-237-6	£17.99	Wiltshire Churches (pb)	1-85937-171-x	£9.99
Plymouth	1-85937-119-1	£12.99	Wiltshire Living Memories	1-85937-245-7	£14.99
Poole & Sandbanks (pb)	1-85937-251-1	£9.99	Winchester (pb)	1-85937-428-x	£9.99
Preston (pb)	1-85937-212-0	£9.99	Windmills & Watermills	1-85937-242-2	£17.99
Reading (pb)	1-85937-238-4	£9.99	Worcester (pb)	1-85937-165-5	£9.99
Romford (pb)	1-85937-319-4	£9.99	Worcestershire	1-85937-152-3	£14.99
Salisbury (pb)	1-85937-239-2	£9.99	York (pb)	1-85937-199-x	£9.99
Scarborough (pb)	1-85937-379-8	£9.99	Yorkshire (pb)	1-85937-186-8	£9.99
St Albans (pb)	1-85937-341-0	£9.99	Yorkshire Living Memories	1-85937-166-3	£14.99

See Frith books on the internet www.francisfrith.co.uk

FRITH PRODUCTS & SERVICES

Francis Frith would doubtless be pleased to know that the pioneering publishing venture he started in 1860 still continues today. A hundred and forty years later, The Francis Frith Collection continues in the same innovative tradition and is now one of the foremost publishers of vintage photographs in the world. Some of the current activities include:

Interior Decoration

Today Frith's photographs can be seen framed and as giant wall murals in thousands of pubs, restaurants, hotels, banks, retail stores and other public buildings throughout the country. In every case they enhance the unique local atmosphere of the places they depict and provide reminders of gentler days in an increasingly busy and frenetic world.

Product Promotions

Frith products are used by many major companies to promote the sales of their own products or to reinforce their own history and heritage. Frith promotions have been used by Hovis bread, Courage beers, Scots Porage Oats, Colman's mustard, Cadbury's foods, Mellow Birds coffee, Dunhill pipe tobacco, Guinness, and Bulmer's Cider.

Genealogy and Family History

As the interest in family history and roots grows world-wide, more and more people are turning to Frith's photographs of Great Britain for images of the towns, villages and streets where their ancestors lived; and, of course, photographs of the churches and chapels where their ancestors were christened, married and buried are an essential part of every genealogy tree and family album.

Frith Products

All Frith photographs are available Framed or just as Mounted Prints and Posters (size 23 x 16 inches). These may be ordered from the address below. From time to time other products - Address Books, Calendars, Table Mats, etc - are available.

The Internet

Already twenty thousand Frith photographs can be viewed and purchased on the internet through the Frith websites and a myriad of partner sites.

For more detailed information on Frith companies and products, look at these sites:

www.francisfrith.co.uk
www.francisfrith.com
(for North American visitors)

See the complete list of Frith Books at:

www.francisfrith.co.uk

This web site is regularly updated with the latest list of publications from the Frith Book Company. If you wish to buy books relating to another part of the country that your local bookshop does not stock, you may purchase on-line.

For further information, trade, or author enquiries please contact us at the address below:
The Francis Frith Collection, Frith's Barn, Teffont, Salisbury, Wiltshire, England SP3 5QP.
Tel: +44 (0)1722 716 376 Fax: +44 (0)1722 716 881   Email: sales@francisfrith.co.uk

See Frith books on the internet www.francisfrith.co.uk

TO RECEIVE YOUR **FREE** MOUNTED PRINT

Mounted Print
Overall size 14 x 11 inches

Cut out this Voucher and return it with your remittance for £1.95 to cover postage and handling, to UK addresses. For overseas addresses please include £4.00 post and handling. Choose any photograph included in this book. Your SEPIA print will be A4 in size, and mounted in a cream mount with burgundy rule line, overall size 14 x 11 inches.

Order additional Mounted Prints at HALF PRICE (only £7.49 each*)

If there are further pictures you would like to order, possibly as gifts for friends and family, purchase them at half price (no additional postage and handling required).

Have your Mounted Prints framed*

For an additional £14.95 per print you can have your chosen Mounted Print framed in an elegant polished wood and gilt moulding, overall size 16 x 13 inches (no additional postage and handling required).

---

* IMPORTANT!
These special prices are only available if ordered using the original voucher on this page (no copies permitted) and at the same time as your free Mounted Print, for delivery to the same address

---

Frith Collectors' Guild

From time to time we publish a magazine of news and stories about Frith photographs and further special offers of Frith products. If you would like 12 months FREE membership, please return this form.

Send completed forms to:
The Francis Frith Collection, Frith's Barn, Teffont, Salisbury, Wiltshire SP3 5QP

Voucher for **FREE** and Reduced Price Frith Prints

Picture no.	Page number	Qty	Mounted @ £7.49	Framed + £14.95	Total Cost
		1	**Free of charge***	£	£
			£7.49	£	£
			£7.49	£	£
			£7.49	£	£
			£7.49	£	£
			£7.49	£	£

Please allow 28 days for delivery	*** Post & handling**	**£1.95**
Book Title	**Total Order Cost**	**£**

Please do not photocopy this voucher. Only the original is valid, so please cut it out and return it to us.

I enclose a cheque / postal order for £ . . . .
made payable to 'The Francis Frith Collection'
OR please debit my Mastercard / Visa / Switch / Amex card
(credit cards please on all overseas orders)

Number . . . .

Issue No (Switch only) . . . . .Valid from (Amex/Switch) . . . .

Expires . . . . Signature . . . .

Name Mr/Mrs/Ms . . . .

Address . . . .

. . . .

. . . . Postcode . . . .

Daytime Tel No . . . .   Valid to 31/12/03

The Francis Frith Collectors' Guild

Please enrol me as a member for 12 months free of charge.

Name Mr/Mrs/Ms . . . .

Address . . . .

. . . .

. . . . Postcode . . . .

Would you like to find out more about Francis Frith?

We have recently recruited some entertaining speakers who are happy to visit local groups, clubs and societies to give an illustrated talk documenting Frith's travels and photographs. If you are a member of such a group and are interested in hosting a presentation, we would love to hear from you.

Our speakers bring with them a small selection of our local town and county books, together with sample prints. They are happy to take orders. A small proportion of the order value is donated to the group who have hosted the presentation. The talks are therefore an excellent way of fundraising for small groups and societies.

Can you help us with information about any of the Frith photographs in this book?

We are gradually compiling an historical record for each of the photographs in the Frith archive. It is always fascinating to find out the names of the people shown in the pictures, as well as insights into the shops, buildings and other features depicted.

If you recognize anyone in the photographs in this book, or if you have information not already included in the author's caption, do let us know. We would love to hear from you, and will try to publish it in future books or articles.

Our production team

Frith books are produced by a small dedicated team at offices in the converted Grade II listed 18th-century barn at Teffont near Salisbury, illustrated above. Most have worked with the Frith Collection for many years. All have in common one quality: they have a passion for the Frith Collection. The team is constantly expanding, but currently includes:

Jason Buck, John Buck, Douglas Burns, Heather Crisp, Lucy Elcock, Isobel Hall, Rob Hames, Hazel Heaton, Peter Horne, James Kinnear, Tina Leary, Hannah Marsh, Eliza Sackett, Terence Sackett, Sandra Sanger, Lewis Taylor, Shelley Tolcher, Helen Vimpany, Clive Wathen and Jenny Wathen.